j808.1
F724

DETROIT PUBLIC LIBRARY

3 ⚹ ⚹ P9-ASD-778

026566928

DETROIT PUBLIC LIBRARY

CHILDREN'S LIBRARY

DATE DUE

MAR 1 6 1999

MAR 3 1 2001

BC-3

AFZ 9945-001

food fight

food

EDiTeD AnD iLLuSTRaTeD bY

fiGht

POEts Join tHE FiGhT aGainsT HunGer

witH POEms TO FaVOriTE FOODs

MiChAeL J. RoSeN

HarCouRt BraCe & COMPanY

san diego   new york   london

J 808.1 F724

Compilation and additional text copyright ©1996 by Michael J. Rosen
Illustrations copyright © 1996 by Michael J. Rosen
"A Word about Good Food" copyright © 1996 by J. Patrick Lewis
"Sunday O Sunday" copyright © 1996 by Mimi Brodsky Chenfeld
"Soft-Boiled Eggs with Boats" copyright © 1996 by Gardner McFall
"Roast Beast Battle" copyright © 1996 by Anne LeMieux
"Mussels in April" copyright © 1996 by Peter Neumeyer
"Pretzels in the Park" copyright © 1996 by Joanne Ryder
"Matzo Ball Soup" copyright © 1996 by Douglas Florian
"Chocolate" copyright © 1996 by Jane Yolen
"Grandma Louise's Gingerbread" copyright ©1996 by Crescent Dragonwagon
"Pineapple Surprise" copyright © 1996 by Nikki Grimes
"Grandma's Scones" copyright © 1996 by Robert San Souci
"The Chocolate Cake" copyright © 1996 by William Jay Smith
"The Picnic Place" copyright © 1996 by Karla Kuskin
"Christmas Cookies" copyright © 1996 by Myra Cohn Livingston
"Artijoke" copyright © 1996 by William Cole
"Pasta Parade" copyright © 1996 by Bobbi Katz
"Salad Haiku" copyright © 1996 by W. Nicola-Lisa
"For a Super Soup-Bean Supper" copyright © 1996 by George Ella Lyon
"Corn: A Hymn" copyright © 1996 by Paul Fleischman
"Summer, Fall, Winter, Spring" copyright © 1996 by Charlotte Zolotow
"Eating Crocodiles" copyright © 1996 by Pat Mora
"Lunch Time" copyright © 1996 by Lee Bennett Hopkins
"Maple-Sugaring Moon" copyright © 1996 by Joseph Bruchac
"Roasting Pumpkin Seeds" copyright © 1996 by X. J. Kennedy
"Eating Alphabet Soup" copyright © 1996 by J. Patrick Lewis
"Battle in the Fjords of Porridge" copyright © 1996 by Peter Neumeyer
"Riddle" copyright © 1996 by Elizabeth Spires
"Hero Sandwich" copyright © 1996 by David Elliott
"The Fruit Bowl" copyright © 1996 by Liz Rosenberg
"Pies: A Lament" copyright © 1996 by James Howe
"August Ice-Cream Cone Poem" copyright © 1996 by Paul Janeczko
"Lunch with Lou" copyright © 1996 by Lois Duncan
"Vegetable Medley" copyright © 1996 by Steven Bauer
"Liquid Poems" copyright © 1996 by Karla Kuskin
"Blackberrying" copyright © 1996 by Crescent Dragonwagon
"Tomato Harvest" copyright © 1996 by Robert San Souci
"Kumquats" copyright © 1996 by Marilyn Singer
"Dreams" copyright © 1996 by Myra Cohn Livingston

All rights reserved. No part of this publication may be reproduced or transmitted in any
form or by any means, electronic or mechanical, including photocopy, recording, or any information
storage and retrieval system, without permission in writing from the publisher.

Requests for permission to make copies of any part of the work should be mailed to: Permissions Department,
Harcourt Brace & Company, 6277 Sea Harbor Drive, Orlando, Florida 32887-6777.

"A Pizza the Size of the Sun," copyright © 1994 by Jack Prelutsky, previously appeared in
Instructor magazine and is used by permission of the author.

Library of Congress Cataloging-in-Publication Data
Food fight: poets join the fight against hunger with poems to
favorite foods/illustrated by Michael J. Rosen.
p.   cm.
Summary: Thirty-three poets, including Lee Bennett Hopkins, Douglas Florian, and Jane Yolen,
write poetry about their favorite foods to help fight against hunger.
ISBN 0-15-201065-3
1. Food—Poetry. 2. American poetry. [1. Food—Poetry. 2. American poetry—Collections.]
I. Rosen, Michael J., 1954– ill.
PS595.F65F66 1996
811′.54080355—dc20 95-37919

First edition

A C E F D B

Printed in Singapore

The illustrations in this book were done in watercolor and ink.
The display type was hand-lettered by Michael J. Rosen.
The text type was set in Schneidler by Thompson Type, San Diego, California.
Color separations by Bright Arts, Ltd., Singapore
Printed and bound by Tien Wah Press, Singapore
This book was printed with soya-based inks on Cougar Opaque wood-free paper.
Production supervision by Warren Wallerstein and Pascha Gerlinger
Designed by Lisa Peters

Contents

Introduction

Welcome to *Food Fight,* a collection of new poems that celebrate the goodness—the greatness!—of good food.

No, this isn't the sort of food fight that once in a while breaks out in the school lunchroom. No tossed carrot sticks, high-flying fish sticks, or catapulted peas. There's a different fight taking place in these pages. Thirty-three American poets have each chosen among the favorite foods of childhood, holidays, garden harvests, or family rituals, proclaimed one the winner, and written a tribute.

Really, there *is* no battle here; food, if anything, is peacetime. The making or sharing of food brings family or new friends together, bridges differences and difficult times, celebrates the passing of traditions as well as years—it teaches, nurtures, and comforts. Along with pleasing our taste buds and fueling our bodies, the acts of breaking bread, dishing out seconds, and giving thanks at meals are among our most human and humane acts—those of generosity, celebration, and commitment.

But there's an even more important fight being waged right now, and the poets in this book have joined in. It's the fight against hunger, a fight waged by one of every twelve elementary school children in America. By offering their talents and donating a poem to this book, the poets here have joined Share Our Strength (SOS), one of the nation's largest antihunger organizations, which sends money to thousands of schools throughout the country so students—nearly half a million—don't have to start the day hungry. SOS has funded more than eight hundred agencies; its work supports a medical van that travels into urban areas to treat malnourished children, a farm near Boston where kids come to grow vegetables for homeless families, and programs that provide food for children during summers, when school lunches aren't available and food bank shelves are empty.

So you see why we wouldn't want to waste real food in this food fight. The fight against hunger is real enough for far too many people. On behalf of all those this book will help, let me add a note of grace before you dig into this smorgasbord of foods and poems— a toast, even: Here's to both good eating and good reading, which we all—every one of us gathered here at this world-over table—we all deserve.

Michael J. Rosen

food
fight

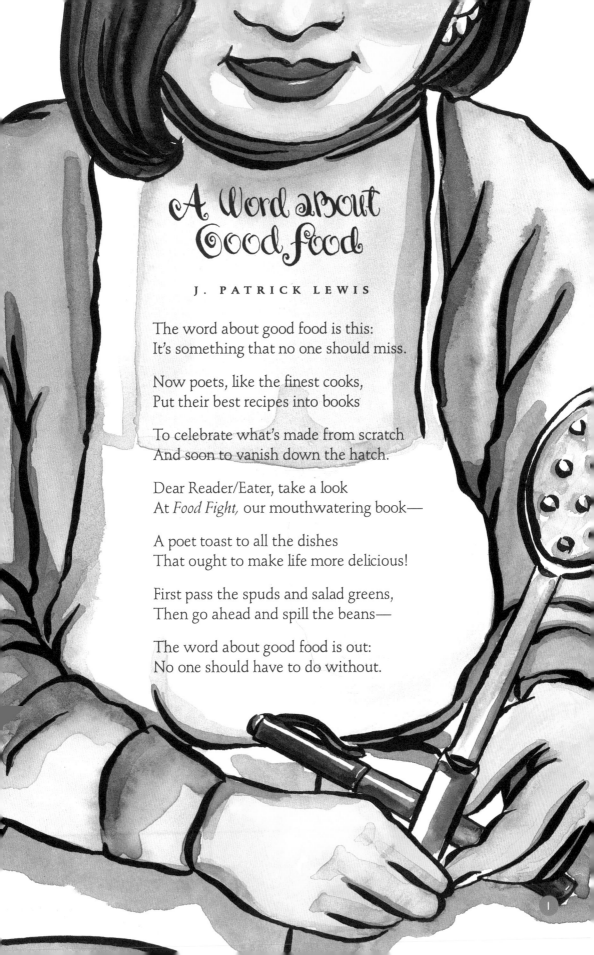

A Word about Good Food

J. PATRICK LEWIS

The word about good food is this:
It's something that no one should miss.

Now poets, like the finest cooks,
Put their best recipes into books

To celebrate what's made from scratch
And soon to vanish down the hatch.

Dear Reader/Eater, take a look
At *Food Fight,* our mouthwatering book—

A poet toast to all the dishes
That ought to make life more delicious!

First pass the spuds and salad greens,
Then go ahead and spill the beans—

The word about good food is out:
No one should have to do without.

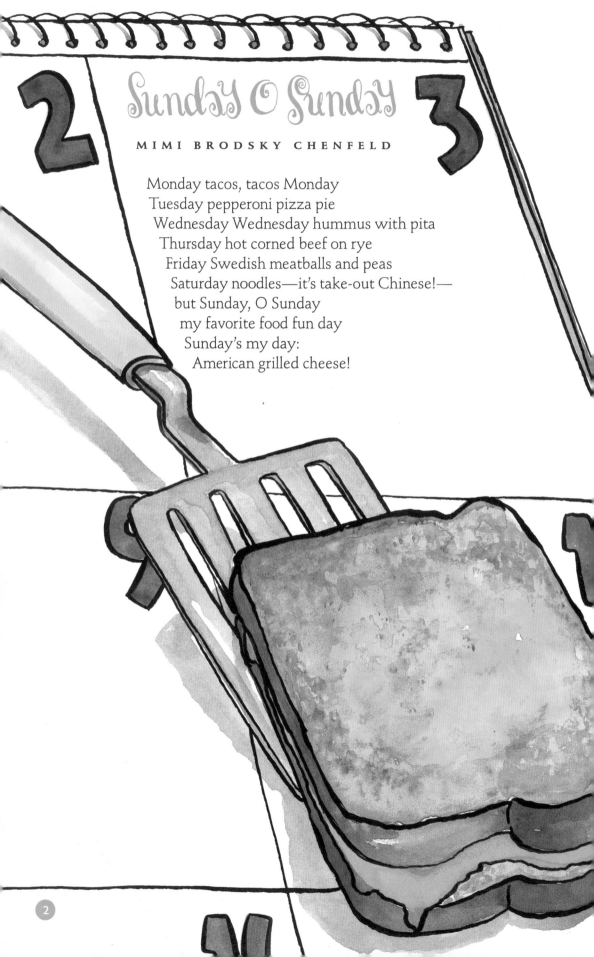

Sunday O Sunday

MIMI BRODSKY CHENFELD

Monday tacos, tacos Monday
Tuesday pepperoni pizza pie
Wednesday Wednesday hummus with pita
Thursday hot corned beef on rye
Friday Swedish meatballs and peas
Saturday noodles—it's take-out Chinese!—
but Sunday, O Sunday
my favorite food fun day
Sunday's my day:
American grilled cheese!

Soft-Boiled Eggs with Boats

GARDNER McFALL

Of all the ways to cook an egg—
scrambled, fried, coddled, poached,
deviled, hard-boiled, shirred—
my favorite's soft-boiled eggs with boats.

It's not a dish you're apt to find
on menus in a restaurant,
and room service is sure to ask,
What kind of egg is that you want?

Please bring two soft-boiled eggs,
I say, and a plate of buttered toast.
I'll gladly show you how I make
my soft-boiled eggs with boats.

First, scoop the eggs into a cup,
then tear the toast without delay
in little pieces. Watch them float:
those toasty boats on an eggy bay

will help you sail into the day!

Roast Beast Battle

ANNE LeMIEUX

The Dark Knight rides with carrot lance,
black olive helmet on his head.
Towards the castle he advances,
coursing o'er ramparts of bread.
  Fork the mashed potatoes higher!
  Up the drawbridge! Fill the moat!
  Brown and muddy as a mire,
  A flood pours from the gravy boat.
Now the Dark Knight presses harder,
gallops on his knuckle-steed.
Will he stop if I bombard him?
Ammunition's what I need.

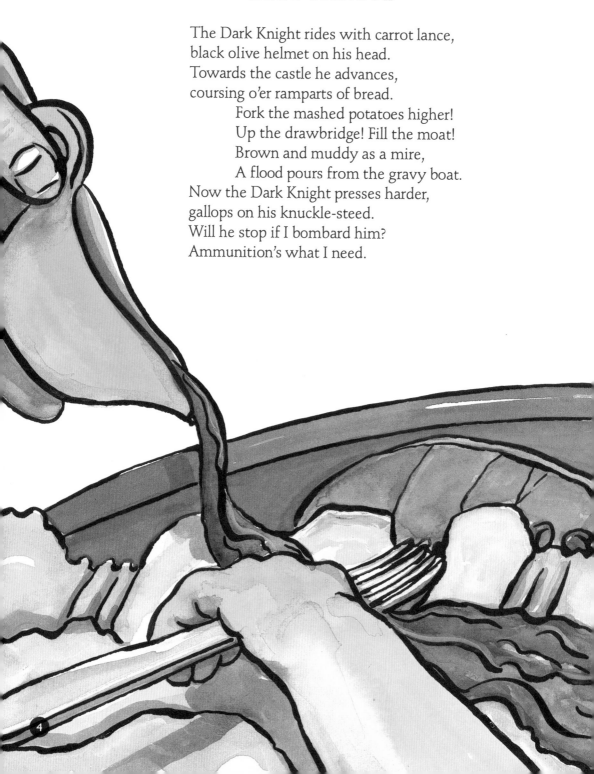

Arm the deadly catapult!
Load the spoon! "Could someone please . . ."
—This should make the villain halt—
". . . pass me down the bowl of peas?"
I raise my hand prepared to wield
The weapon, but Queen Mom proclaims,
"This dinner's not a battlefield!
You eat your food and stop the games!"
One quick crunch, the Dark Knight falls!
Now the Battle of Roast Beast
—*Mmmm,* I love mashed castle walls!—
becomes my tasty victory feast!

Mussels in April

PETER NEUMEYER

"All months with R," my father said
So
    —come April, wearing slip-proof Keds
we'd leap the rocks,
start up the squawking gulls,
crouch, wrench, twist the bearded blueblack treasures
streaked with silver.
Once home, we'd turn the pail, discard the open,
simmer in seaweed and their own salt tears
those sealed mysteries till they gapped
and through the smallest slit, their golden eyes
    would squint.
These family moments—cold outings, simmering pots,
scraped fingers, salty steam, the clickclack shells—
these rituals to my children I'll pass on;
and they'll do likewise when I'm gone.

Pretzels in the Park

JOANNE RYDER

Near the icy pond,
a weathered man warms
golden twists of bread.
Papa asks for two,
picking the smaller for himself.
My words of thanks
spread in a chilly cloud
before my face.
I break the corners
into crusty smiles,
and lick my fingers
flecked with white,
tasting the salt,
melting, melting . . .
Papa finishes his treat,
but fluffed-up pigeons
circle near my feet.
Carefully, I tear apart
a ragged loop, the last,
scattering as many pieces
as I can to share with them.

Matzo Ball Soup

DOUGLAS FLORIAN

All alone or with a group
I love eating matzo ball soup.
I will beg, cajole, or stoop
To be near my matzo ball soup.
Made from matzo, tastes good hotza.
Watch me slurp it, swallow, burp it.
Every bowlful makes me soulful.
Palest yellow, smooth and mellow.
Soft and mushy, always cushy.
Slightly spicy, starts meals nicely.
Stirring!
Steaming!
Sends me dreaming!
Scheming, screaming!
Give me lotza
Pots and potza
Matzo ball soup!

CHOCOLATE

JANE YOLEN

I am an eater, no doubt.
There's hardly a food I'll leave out.
I eat all sorts of greenery—
Lettuce to beanery.
Meat, fish, and chickens
Are my kind of pickin's.
As for pizza, potpies,
Parfaits, pretzels, French fries—
If it's salty or sweet,
Then I'll eat.

But chocolate.
Oh—chocolate.
If it starts as cacao
I'll practically sway, oh—
I'll faint, I'll fall senseless,
I'll swooooooooon.
Just find me a plate
Or a platter (serves eight)
And my own
Giant-sized serving spoon.

Grandma Louise's Gingerbread

CRESCENT DRAGONWAGON

Grandmama made gingerbread—
her writing's on this card—
her recipe in curled black script
directs, "Don't beat too hard."

My mother ate it after school
cut in a warm brown square
when she was just a little girl,
and Grandmama was there.

Sugar, egg, and buttermilk,
molasses, ginger, flour—
mix and measure, put to bake
only half an hour.

I never met my grandmama
and never will (she's dead),
but I kind of know her, since
I eat her gingerbread.

Gingerbread
molasses   egg
flour
sugar   ginger

Pineapple Surprise

NIKKI GRIMES

Grandma wasn't much for hugging.
She was entirely too frail
to give me piggyback rides
and moved too slow
for hide-and-seek.
But, sometimes,
while I played alone,
she would magically appear
with pineapple upside-down cake,
which took considerable time to make:

Honey-glazed pineapple rings
clinging to the bottom—
or was it the top?
Maraschino cherries pop-
ping with tooth-tingling
tangy sweetness,
two thick layers of buttery,
gooey, scrumptiously chewy,
pineapple-licious yellow cake
baked for nobody else but me.

Grandma's Scones

ROBERT D. SAN SOUCI

"I came to California when I turned seventeen.
Before, I'd never left my town of Skibereen.
But across the miles," my grandma said, "all on my own,
Ireland would return in every taste of every scone."

I'd visit and she'd butter scones and pour us tea,
And tell of growing up an orphan in a village by the sea.
Emerald hills and golden shores by lakes of bluest silk
Were treasures for that scullery girl eating bread-and-milk.

Best was Sunday evening, when the old folks told their stories
Of heroes and high kings and all of Ireland's glories.
They spoke, as well, of children lost to fairy mounds
And warned: Beware of banshees, for death is in their sounds.

"We ate our scones enraptured," my grandma would recall.
"One bite brings back those days as if I hadn't left at all."
And though I'd never been there, like magic, scones and tea
Carried me to bright-dark Ireland and that village by the sea.

Crusty outside, inside light and sweet as sugared air,
Each was tastier for the countless currants hidden there.
All these years later, when I have a scone with tea,
I'm back where Grandma regales a younger, spellbound me.

The Chocolate Cake

WILLIAM JAY SMITH

Mother decided once to bake
A huge delicious chocolate cake.
How nice of Mother to prepare it!
I asked my friends to come and share it.
They said they would, but they were late,
And so I had to sit and wait.

Their forks were laid out on the table,
And round the cake each empty chair
Sat in gloomy silence there
Until at last I thought I might
Dare to take a little bite.
And so I did, and then another . . .
And moments later, still another . . .

Then when my friends knocked at the door,
The cake that was
                              was there no more.

(adapted from a Russian poem by Daniil Kharms)

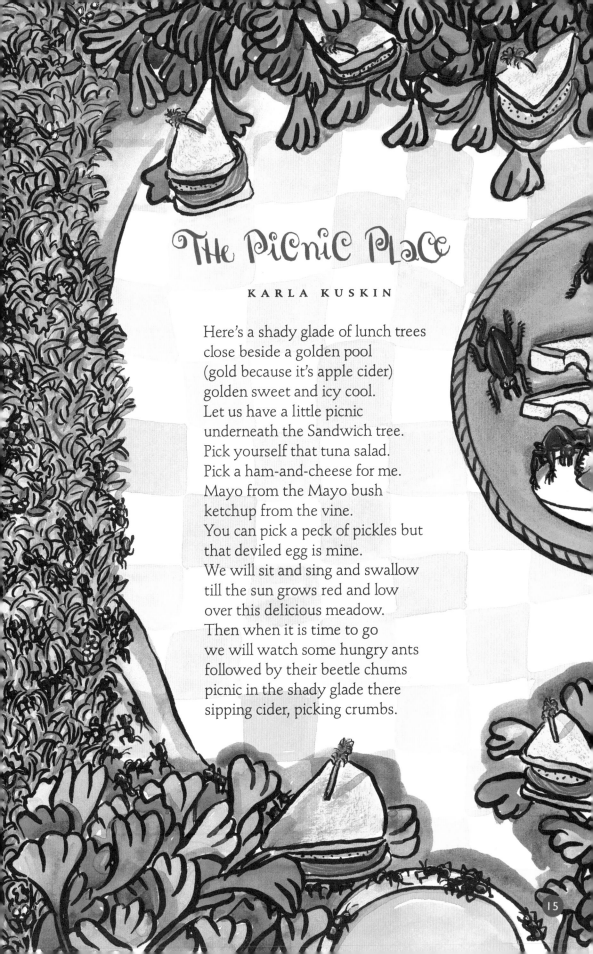

THE PICNIC PLACE

KARLA KUSKIN

Here's a shady glade of lunch trees
close beside a golden pool
(gold because it's apple cider)
golden sweet and icy cool.
Let us have a little picnic
underneath the Sandwich tree.
Pick yourself that tuna salad.
Pick a ham-and-cheese for me.
Mayo from the Mayo bush
ketchup from the vine.
You can pick a peck of pickles but
that deviled egg is mine.
We will sit and sing and swallow
till the sun grows red and low
over this delicious meadow.
Then when it is time to go
we will watch some hungry ants
followed by their beetle chums
picnic in the shady glade there
sipping cider, picking crumbs.

Christmas Cookies

MYRA COHN LIVINGSTON

Reindeer, stars, bells, Christmas trees—
all the cookies look like these

baked for Christmas, cut from dough,
frosted, sugared. Who will know

where we licked when icing dripped
and somehow Blitzen's tail got nipped?

Who will guess we ate the bell
with chocolate sprinkles? Who can tell

we cut four stars a little thin
to put inside the cookie tin

so let's give Jennifer a taste.
Still, there's too much to go to waste

so you have this—the frosting's fine!
And now that you're through tasting mine

I'll take a bite of your blue star.
You go and find the cookie jar

while I save three bells out because
we should leave some for Santa Claus,

and then we'll put the rest away
so we can eat them Christmas Day.

A Pizza the Size of the Sun

JACK PRELUTSKY

I'm making a pizza the size of the sun,
a pizza that's sure to weigh more than a ton,
a pizza too massive to pick up and toss,
a pizza resplendent with oceans of sauce.

I'm topping my pizza with mountains of cheese,
with acres of peppers, pimentos, and peas,
with mushrooms, tomatoes, and sausage galore,
with every last olive they had at the store.

My pizza is sure to be one of a kind,
   my pizza will leave other pizzas behind,
      my pizza will be a delectable treat
         that all who love pizza are welcome to eat.

The oven is hot, I believe it will take
a year and a half for my pizza to bake—
I hardly can wait till my pizza is done,
my wonderful pizza the size of the sun.

Artijoke

WILLIAM COLE

The artichoke's a funny food,
'Cause when you've finished one,
You'll have much more upon your plate
Than when you had begun!

Pasta Parade

BOBBI KATZ

Ziti marching in a row—
then capelli d'angelo—
ravioli—
tortellini—
wide lasagna—
slim linguine—
itty bits of pert pastina—
piles of penne mezzanine—
ditali and ditalini—
teeny, weeny tubettini—
farfalle—
and capellini—
nests of woven fettuccine—
Basta!
That's enough already,
Fill my bowl up with spaghetti!
And while you're at it, will you please
pass along the grated cheese.

Salad Haiku

W. NICOLA-LISA

On this leafy bed
slices of cucumber sleep,
cold as winter dimes.

Tomatoes will squish
no matter how you cut them.
Even prayers won't help.

Spinach comes with dirt!
That's just how it is sometimes—
good and bad in one.

Whether whole or sliced,
olives sink like submarines,
and will not surface.

Red onions or white?
It doesn't matter to me—
crying is crying!

For a Super Soup-Bean Supper

GEORGE ELLA LYON

Take   hundreds of things
thousands of things
look 'em and poke 'em
soak 'em and cook 'em
with sowbelly meat
to make the soup sweet

Get   a cast-iron skillet
make batter to fill it

Mix   cornmeal   buttermilk
soda   egg   salt
bacon grease   baking powder
can't find fault
with a pone of journey cake
made just for the sake
of all those soup beans

'cause strange as it seems
most of my kin grows
on big bowls of pintos
and rich golden rounds
of grown from the ground
corn. I say, corn. Corn bread!

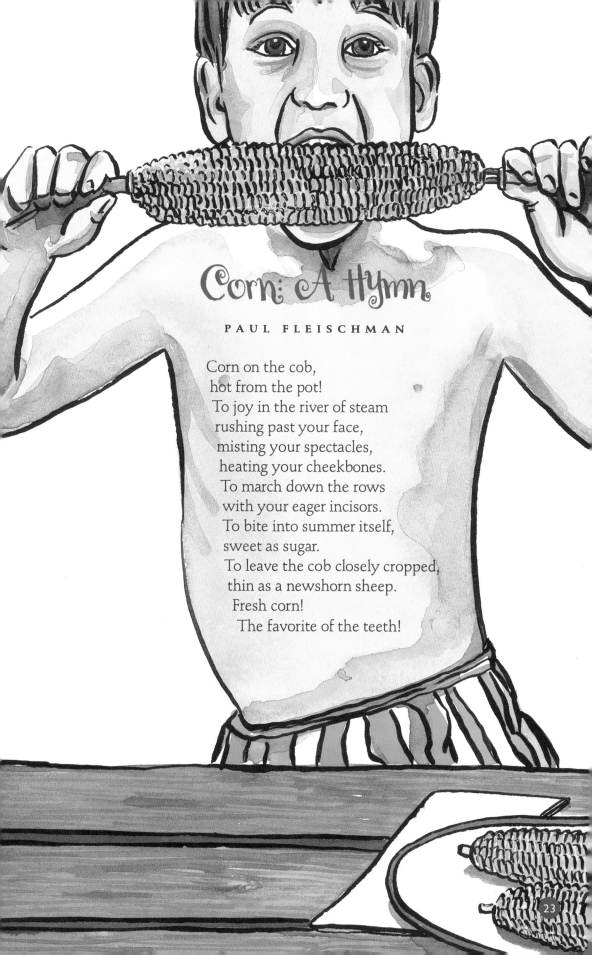

Corn: A Hymn

PAUL FLEISCHMAN

Corn on the cob,
hot from the pot!
To joy in the river of steam
rushing past your face,
misting your spectacles,
heating your cheekbones.
To march down the rows
with your eager incisors.
To bite into summer itself,
sweet as sugar.
To leave the cob closely cropped,
thin as a newshorn sheep.
Fresh corn!
The favorite of the teeth!

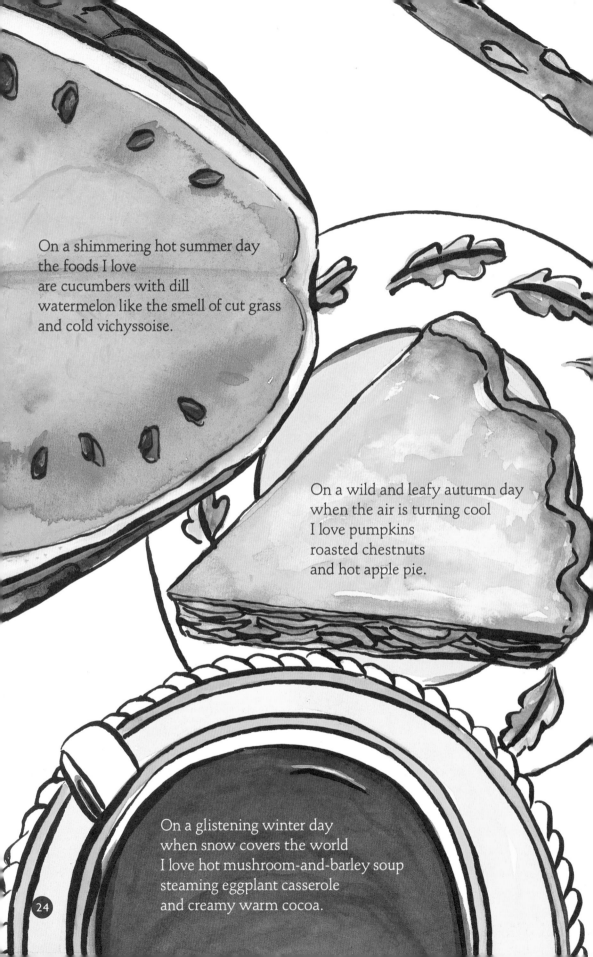

On a shimmering hot summer day
the foods I love
are cucumbers with dill
watermelon like the smell of cut grass
and cold vichyssoise.

On a wild and leafy autumn day
when the air is turning cool
I love pumpkins
roasted chestnuts
and hot apple pie.

On a glistening winter day
when snow covers the world
I love hot mushroom-and-barley soup
steaming eggplant casserole
and creamy warm cocoa.

Summer, fall, Winter, Spring

CHARLOTTE ZOLOTOW

And in the softness of spring
I love leafy salad, slender asparagus
and cool light custard
pale as springtime sunlight,
                          and as sweet.

Eating Crocodiles

PAT MORA

Coconut mountains,
sticky chocolate bricks,
sugar lava spilling
down a bread volcano,
metal platters of *pan dulce*
at my neighborhood *panadería,*
edible *libritos*
with pages of papery dough.
Our friend, the *panadero,* hands us
cinnamon and anise trees,
stars, leaves, *nopalitos,*
and makes his cookie zoo,
swans, shrimp, turtles, worms too,
the room warmed by the aroma
of *marranitos* swollen with brown sugar.
We lick crumbs of a crisp crocodile
sweet on our lips.

LunCH Time

LEE BENNETT HOPKINS

Oh, for a piece of papaya,
or a plate of beef lo mein—

Oh, for a bowl of Irish stew,
or fresh paella from Spain—

Oh, for a forkful of couscous,
or a chunk of Jarlsberg cheese—

Oh, for some lasagna,
or a bowl of black-eyed peas—

Of all the tasty foods
That I would love to try,

I sit here and wonder
why, oh why,
Mama packed me
this liverwurst on rye.

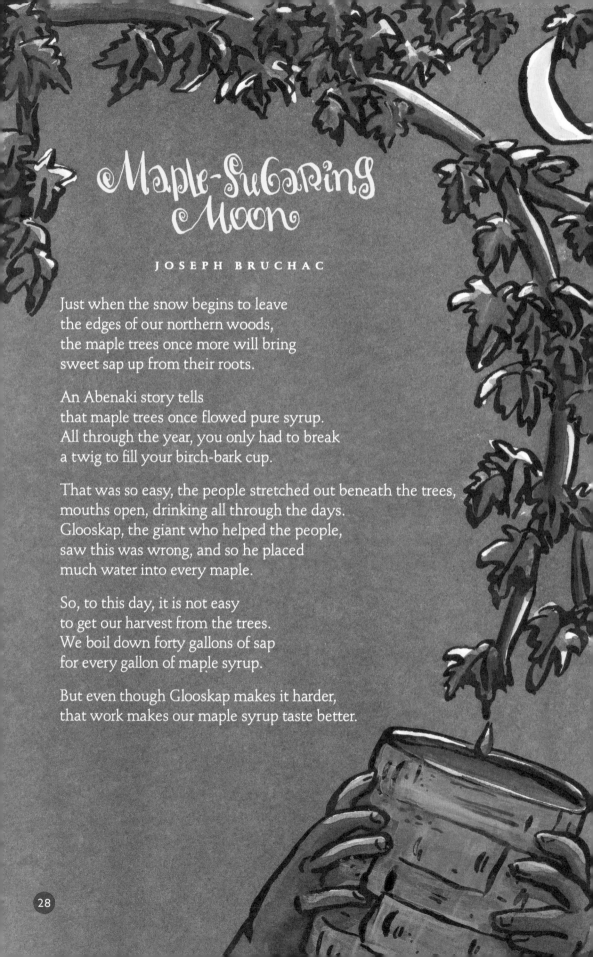

Maple-Sugaring Moon

JOSEPH BRUCHAC

Just when the snow begins to leave
the edges of our northern woods,
the maple trees once more will bring
sweet sap up from their roots.

An Abenaki story tells
that maple trees once flowed pure syrup.
All through the year, you only had to break
a twig to fill your birch-bark cup.

That was so easy, the people stretched out beneath the trees,
mouths open, drinking all through the days.
Glooskap, the giant who helped the people,
saw this was wrong, and so he placed
much water into every maple.

So, to this day, it is not easy
to get our harvest from the trees.
We boil down forty gallons of sap
for every gallon of maple syrup.

But even though Glooskap makes it harder,
that work makes our maple syrup taste better.

Roasting Pumpkin Seeds

X. J. KENNEDY

To carve a pumpkin, lift its lid—
    Inside, it's moist and mucky.
You wonder how will you get rid
    Of such a mess of yucky

Stretched strings like slimy rubber bands?
    The seeds, they're what you save.
So roll your sleeves up, plunge your hands
    Right through its brains. Be brave!

You wash the guck off, line with foil
    A big flat baking pan,
Turn oven on, drench seeds in oil,
    And toast 'em till they tan.

A shake of salt? That just might help.
    Don't burn 'em, don't ignite 'em.
They'll come out blazing hot—don't yelp—
    Count ten before you bite 'em.

They'd be a hard thing to improve.
    What's more, on Halloween night
By taking all those seeds out, you've
    Made room for candlelight!

Eating Alphabet Soup

J. PATRICK LEWIS

My advice to the Tablespoon Slurper:
Beware what you do with that scoop!
    The Capitals, sir,
    Can cause quite a stir
In a bowlful of Alphabet Soup.

When K, Z, and B do the backstroke
Across this hot, steamy lagoon,
    The fun-loving Vowels
    May want tiny towels
To dry themselves off on the spoon.

But when Letters go swimming together
In sentences, nothing can beat
    The pleasure of reading
    The food that you're eating!
So dive in and—*bon appétit!*

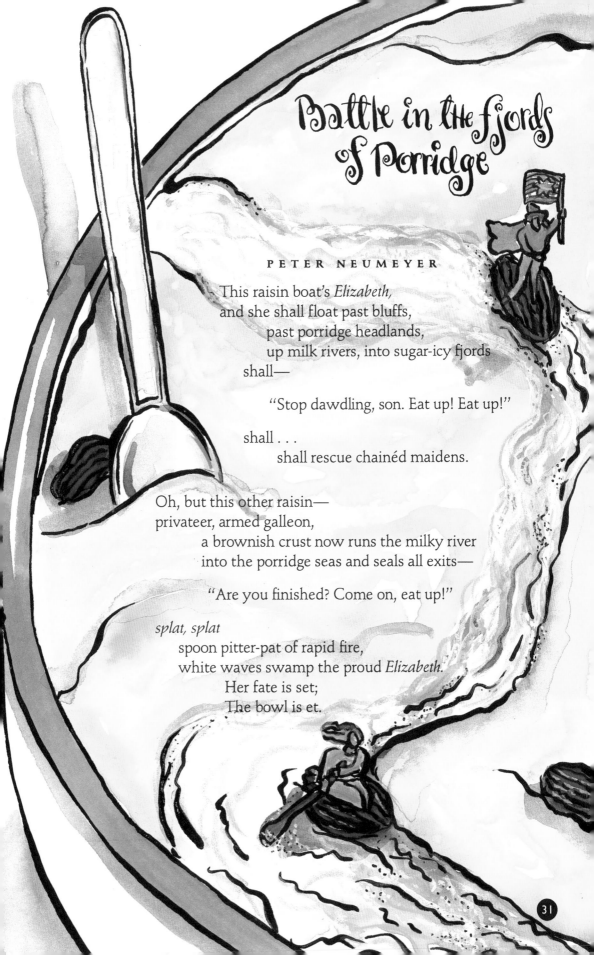

Battle in the Fjords of Porridge

PETER NEUMEYER

This raisin boat's *Elizabeth*,
and she shall float past bluffs,
    past porridge headlands,
    up milk rivers, into sugar-icy fjords
shall—

    "Stop dawdling, son. Eat up! Eat up!"

    shall . . .
        shall rescue chainéd maidens.

Oh, but this other raisin—
privateer, armed galleon,
    a brownish crust now runs the milky river
    into the porridge seas and seals all exits—

    "Are you finished? Come on, eat up!"

splat, splat
    spoon pitter-pat of rapid fire,
    white waves swamp the proud *Elizabeth*.
        Her fate is set;
        The bowl is et.

Riddle

ELIZABETH SPIRES

Three sat down at the table.
Two worked together while the third watched.
There was a stabbing, a robbery, and a cut throat.
When the maid walked in, the third jumped in the soup.
Taken away, they were judged not guilty.
Tomorrow they'll be at it again.

Hero Sandwich

DAVID A. ELLIOTT

Start at ground zero when making a hero,
which means with a bun or a roll.
The philosopher Hegel said, "Don't use a bagel!
The good stuff all falls out the hole!"

Do as you please when it comes to the cheese—
Swiss, provolone, one of those.
I'd recommend cheddar, but Limburger's better
if you don't mind holding your nose.

Now add the salami, baloney, pastrami;
the ham, by all means, try Bavarian.
Pile on the roast beef! Oh heavens! Good grief!
I forgot you're a strict vegetarian.

Pepper it well, though I think I should tell
you, this practice some find unappealing.
Because if you sneeze, the meat and the cheese
will end up on the floor and the ceiling.

However you do it, be sure that you chew it—
and properly; that's my suggestion,
as it's rather foreboding to feel it exploding
in your upper and lower digestion.

The Fruit Bowl

LIZ ROSENBERG

Banana
Crescent moon
zipped snug in its skin

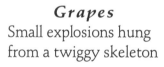

Apple
A round red planet with a star
at its center

Grapes
Small explosions hung
from a twiggy skeleton

Strawberry
The freckle-faced one
who smells like heaven

Peach
The soft skin fuzzy, thin;
like the skin of old women

Pear
A fruit guitar
whose music is nectar

Lemon
Bright as the dawn, but
the taste—don't mention it

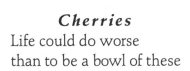

Blueberries
Blue as the dusk,
flavor of musk

Pomegranate
A hive of garnets
inside the red lantern

Cherries
Life could do worse
than to be a bowl of these

Pies: A Lament

JAMES HOWE

"There's something about the flour,"
My mother would always say,
"That made better pies in the past
Than the pie I am making today.

"The crust is crumbly and dry;
It's certain to fall apart.
The filling is runny; it tastes a bit funny.
Too sweet? No, a touch too tart.

"The chocolate isn't quite right;
The apples are wronger than wrong.
The lemons were old to begin with;
The cinnamon's much too strong.

"The banana creme isn't creamy
Enough; the berries are terribly sour.
But the biggest problem by far
Is this awful new-improved flour!"

So, were her pies the worst of the worst?
I'm sure you can fill in the rest:
Of all the pies I have eaten,
Hers were the best of the best!

August
Ice-Cream Cone
Poem

PAUL B. JANECZKO

Lick
quick.

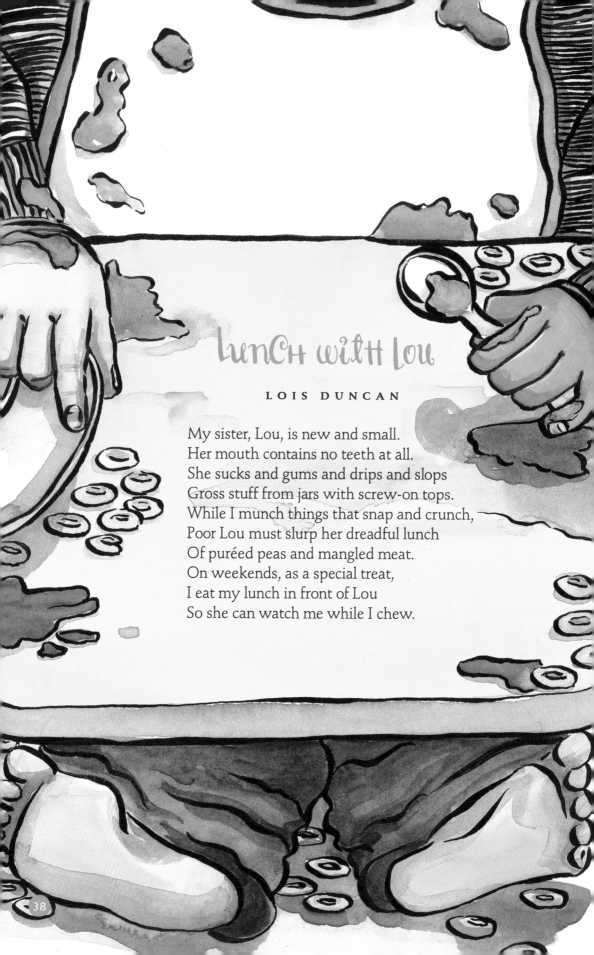

Lunch with Lou

LOIS DUNCAN

My sister, Lou, is new and small.
Her mouth contains no teeth at all.
She sucks and gums and drips and slops
Gross stuff from jars with screw-on tops.
While I munch things that snap and crunch,
Poor Lou must slurp her dreadful lunch
Of puréed peas and mangled meat.
On weekends, as a special treat,
I eat my lunch in front of Lou
So she can watch me while I chew.

Vegetable Medley
(A cHaNt, tO Be sHouTeD, PreFeraBLy)

STEVEN BAUER

I like vegetables—
Carrots and string beans.
And I love broccoli,
Brussels sprouts and greens.

Of all the vegetables,
There's only one I hate,
And I hate lima beans—
I flick them off my plate

When Mom's not looking
And ask to be excused.
(I flush them down the toilet
Or hide them in my shoes.)

But I like vegetables—
Artichokes are neat.
Corn and peas and eggplant,
Asparagus and beets.

Other kids like burgers,
Chocolate shakes, and fries,
But I like vegetables.
Eat them or you'll die.

LiQuiD PoemS

KARLA KUSKIN

Some things you know
and don't need to be told:
the thing about milk is
it's wonderful cold.
But if it sits out in the heat of the sun
for hours on end,
I would like to have none.

Juice is lovely liquid,
orange, apple, pear.
Squeeze some fruit to fill a glass.
Then *gulp, gulp, gulp*
your share.
Ahhh . . . there.

Drinking from a bottle,
drinking from a cup,
the only way to drink a drink
is simply drink it up.

Drinking in the country,
drinking in the town,
the only way to drink a drink
is simply drink it down.

She drank
and added with a frown,
"It's funny,
up tastes just like *down*."

Blackberrying

CRESCENT DRAGONWAGON

the green arched bramble branches hung thick
with blue-black berries,
summer Christmas trees,

catching at us, we bent to pick
(and only our backs got sunburned)
catching at us, scratching (and we got mosquito-bit too)

now there's a shelf full of blackberry jam
and that night, pie

next winter it will be cold
we will spread that sharp sweet dark
on breakfast toast
and think we remember what hot really felt like

and how there was a night (tonight,
remembered) when, after picking, we came home
        and how we made a pie, ate it,
            and laughed ("giddy" Daddy finally called us)
because our teeth,
until we brushed them late late late that hot night,
had all turned
blackberry blue

Tomato Harvest

ROBERT D. SAN SOUCI

What it was I still don't know
That urged a fourth-grade me to grow
Tomatoes in the strip of clay
Not used for planting—just for play.

My brothers laughed and called me dense—
Tomato farming made no sense.
What's more, the place already grew
Lots of sour grass to chew.

I ignored them both, my mind on things
Like hanging foil strips on strings
To keep away the birds that hoped to eat
The seeds fresh-sown in earth and peat.

I watered and weeded those seedlings of mine
Braced the stalks with stakes and twine,
And watched for snails and worms—that bunch
Of pests for whom green leaves mean lunch.

One night it rained so fiercely that
By dawn most plants were beaten flat;
I felt beaten splashing out to see
How little garden was left to me.

Those losses made my harvest small:
One bucketful of fruit was all—
But when I picked my first and tried it,
What sweetness and pride I found inside it.

KumQuats

MARILYN SINGER

At six I sat in red—
    the first dress Mommy let me choose—
      matching the restaurant walls.
On my plate lay sparerib bones
    and dabs of duck sauce:
signs of success at my first real Chinese meal.
Then the waiter, smiling wide, said, "For the little lady,"
    and set before me a dish of kumquats.
"She won't like those," said Mommy.
    And Daddy, he agreed.
So, of course, I dug right in, spearing
    the slippery Halloween-orange fruit with my toothpick,
    biting through the thick syrup-drenched rind
      to the puckery pithy pulp inside.
It was awful. It was grand.
    Bittersoursweet, it tasted of travel,
      of lands I'd never seen.
And now when everyone wants brownies, cookies, or ice cream
    it's kumquats I crave—
      a ticket to adventure,
      a badge of when I was brave.

Dreams

MYRA COHN LIVINGSTON

We dream ice cream,
we dream cake,
brownies, cookies,
freshly baked,
sold from counters
piled high
with Danish,
cupcakes,
apple pie.

We dream hot dogs,
burgers, chips,
French toast,
pancakes,
frozen whips,
éclairs filled with
coffee cream,
candy,
all of this we dream.

When we wake,
when dreams are fed,
we pray to God
for
daily bread.

SHARE OUR STRENGTH (SOS) is one of the nation's leading antihunger organizations, mobilizing industries and individuals—including chefs, poets, and artists—to contribute their talents to fight hunger. Since its founding in 1984, Share Our Strength has distributed more than $26 million in grants to over eight hundred antihunger organizations in the United States, Canada, and developing countries. Through grants to organizations that distribute food, treat the consequences of hunger and malnutrition, and build self-sufficiency, Share Our Strength meets immediate needs for food while investing in long-term solutions to hunger.

For more information about joining the fight against hunger, or for a packet of classroom support materials that includes projects and ideas to extend children's participation in hunger-relief efforts, please contact:

SHARE OUR STRENGTH
1511 K Street NW, Suite 940
Washington, D.C. 20005
1-800-969-4767

e-mail: SOSbooks@aol.com